Lady of the Lake

and other poems on aging parents

John Sokalski

Presentation by *BookLeaf Publishing*

Web: www.bookleafpub.com

E-mail: info@bookleafpub.com

ISBN: 978-93-5761-094-0

First edition 2022

DEDICATION

To my parents, for everything.

ACKNOWLEDGEMENT

To my wife, Cheryl, for making this happen.

Lost Love

My Mother fell in love with a lake.
Introduced by neighbors,
the lake became her summer lover,
giving her deep dives and long canoe rides
while she brought bouquets
of colorfully dressed children
to cast upon its waters.
She moved from the flirtations
of an occasional, nearby rental
to the deep commitment
of a hilltop temple of windows
where she could delight
in its ongoing pageantry.
She dreamed of living there full-time
like the other wild creatures she met
as she endlessly circled its shores.
Her walks forged a ring around the lake
that needed no other ceremony
to declare her love.
In the end, her aging took her away
from her walks, away
from her dreams, away
from her lake lover.

Great Lakes Fever

(after John Masefield)

2

He must go down to the Lakes again, to the restless waves and the sky,
And seek out dreams of ore ships and a following wind to ride,
He knows the routes through narrow locks 'gainst winter's icy hand,
But a grey mist shrouds his face from me, pressing close upon the man.

He must go down to the Lakes again, for the current guides his heart
A call to the child and a call to the man that were never far apart
And all he asks is a clear crisp day for freighter and for sail
To see stout ships, fine crew, and a tug to deliver the mail.

He must go down to the Lakes again, so twined into his soul,
From the railway to the seaway 'til his bell's final toll.
And all I can do is sing a soft shanty with laughter and with tears,
And wish him peaceful voyages as he fades into the years

Ready For Dead

I thought I was ready for dead.

Not being there
I cycled through
Rounds of updates
Crisp, clear electronica

This is what we know
        This is what they say
                This is how he is

I thought I was ready for dead.

Finally, a chance to call my Dad
But hearing his slurred speech
His resignation that "parts wear out"
And his hope to make it to 60 wedded years.

This was a punch to the gut
        This went past all my defenses
                This was nothing I could understand

I thought I was ready for dead.

But only now was it becoming real
What do we know? Facts are not all of reality
What do they say? They deal in mechanism, not person
Who cares how he is? I do.

I want to hold him like he held my child-self
        I want to kiss the top of that sweet, bald head.
                I want to pull out a hankie and wipe away his tears.

I am not ready for dead.

Her Memory Quilt

has become more patchwork,
faded, and frayed
around today's edges.
Whole pieces of time
have been left behind
and she's lost the thread
to hold it all together.
Early patterns of childhood
are smooth and sharp,
but her Granny squares are bunched up,
overlapping, and leaving gaps
that frustrate her to fish-mouthed silence.
Setting them straight
would open new wounds
causing her pointless pain.
The best I can do is wrap her up
in my own memory gently,
matching patterns she taught me,
covering for the holes,
and sharing the warmth
of our shared memories.

The Island of My Father

5

is slowly washing away.
Since the stroke tsunami,
one arm has collapsed inward
of the two that once circled
that calm bay we grew up in,
keeping out the storms and giving hugs.

Time has accelerated
and the broad beach of his belly
where we used to lay
and look up at the mountain
for wisdom or a smile
has sunk into his frame.

The mighty forest of his upright legs
through which we peered and played
has fallen, weathered and graying,
reduced to wheelchair driftwood
moving slowly in the tide.

Each year it gets harder and harder
to swim to that distant shore,
cutting across the concourse currents,
braving the barrier reefs of polite conversation,
skirting emotional riptides.

When I arrive, the accommodations are primitive.
My reservations, set aside, cast away.
I struggle for even the basics,
but oh to watch the son-light in his eyes
with the gentle shush
of his breath upon the shore
and know that I have come home.

The Watchers

Alone together, I am looking
after my parents as they watch
a sparrow land on the perch.

"Bird on the feeder! Bird on the feeder!"
"I see it! I see it!"

I can't take them
anywhere as they watch
someone walking a lab.

"Look at that dog!" "The guy is in shorts!"
"Must be warm out!"

I am always there
for them as they watch
a pigeon fail to land on the feeder.

"Did you see that? Too big to land on the feeder!"
"Only small birds here, buddy!"

I try to connect somehow
with them while they look out
and see a woman with a stroller, and another
sparrow, a dog walker, and a runner go by.
Each gets noticed.
Each gets announced.
I
could
just
SCREAM!
They don't know
the people. They can't identify
the dog breeds. They can barely distinguish
pigeon from sparrow.

They just
Watch
Out the window
And acknowledge
Every living thing
As if it were
A big deal.
As if life
were
A BIG DEAL...

Bird on the feeder! Bird on the feeder!

First To Say Goodbye

I was the first to say goodbye
Day by day,
As frailty
Captured more of your body, your mind, your spirit.

Your world became a building, a room, then continued to shrink
Hour by hour.
Nostalgia
Weighed you down, a rusted anchor to the past.

We children and grandchildren went digital, on line, away
Second by second
Faster
Than you could keep up, or even want to anymore.

You became childlike without youthful promise, living
Moment by moment
Escaping
The now, running from the next, compass spinning blindly.

As you slipped deeper into the sands of history
Grain by grain
Memories
Blurred together, shifted, and drifted out of reach.

I also began to drift away in mind and spirit
Visit by visit
Echoing
Your past from further in my future, missing your fears.

And so I became the first to say goodbye,
Choice by choice
Distancing
Until we were strangers, mannequins mouthing our platitudes until the final
farewell.

Along the Rio Grande

9

I bundle them up with temps in the 70s
Sharp brimmed ball cap for him
Floppy pink flowered hat for her
Pull up to the curb and wheel him out
The careful transition from chair to van
With a hug in the form of buckling him in
She's already in the van and waiting
Buckled and bouncing
She's done this too often it seems
At the park the sun shimmers off the Rio Grande
As I push him along the path
She wanders away and back
The trees are bare
The reeds and grasses brittle
But the sky is an achingly beautiful blue
And the river flows on and on
The three of us chat
Only about what we see
Truly living in the now
They pose for me with portrait smiles
But hands held tight together
Their bodies are pared down
Like the trees and grown brittle
As the hollow reeds, but their eyes
Still shine like sunlight

The Lady of the Lake

Every day I wade in
and try my best to find you.
Immersed in your own world, I catch
your laugh, your smile, shimmering glimpses
of your true self in the peaceful calm of morning.
But the slightest breath of change casts ripples,
repeated distortions blurring your words and any insights
I may have. You respond with rage against the waters
so completely closing you in, fists and eyes clenched in
a sudden flush of red. I cannot stay and must retreat,
seeking safety on calmer shores. As night closes in,
the moon's tidal pull seems to swell and ebb
the distance between us. I wade out further
and further to reach you while I still can.
But in the end I know you'll pass
beyond my grasp.

Words

The words have stopped coming out.
It's not that the words aren't there
exactly,

but it takes so much effort

that often they are mangled

or just wrong

when they finally arrive
falling faint and fluttering

from your lips,
a tired sigh
of sound,

the disappointment

on your face,
clenched brow
reflecting questions,

frustration.

Reduced to nods

and frowns

where once we chatted
at length

in the world of language
you clutch my hand.
With touch, connection.
We both smile
and know
we are loved beyond words.

Hummingbird Heart

Her mouth a silent chasm.
Her hummingbird heart
beating too-fast rhythms
trying to stay aloft
for one final, sweet sip
from the fatal beauty
of this ephemeral life.

Rise and dip,
dart and dash,
her eyes seek without seeing.
Twist and turn,
claw and curl,
her finger talons move
miming memories of motions

or moved by emotions
of pain too hard to bear.
Her hummingbird heart
with its red throated cry
pleads for one more moment
or an end to it all

and suddenly stills.

Iceberg

The loss of a spouse
Destroys your once solid us.
Like an iceberg calving
With a groaning screaming cry
Pieces of your life fall away.
You begin to crack up.
Shared memories drift away, unreachable
As wave upon relentless wave of emotion
Punishes the remains, upending balance
Threatening to take you under.
You float on lopsided, more exposed,
Melting away

Still Life

The old vase clutches a bouquet
of dried flower memories
grown fragile and gray
from black and white thinking
of black and white days
random blooms are missing
while others stand out
worn shiny and smooth
from endless retelling
like the praying of rosary beads

A few sprigs of new greenery
music videos and video calls
adorn the rough edges
cuttings of baby's breath
and other children's tales
add a certain fullness while
crumbling seed pods
of might-have-beens
lay cast aside sacrificed
to his past our future

But I only see the outward facing
two dimensions with hints
of what lay behind
what he allows me to see
I'm not sure how to help
with his final self-portrait
except to pour in a pitcher of time
filling gaps to make memories whole
and add my color commentary to his
still life

No More Tomorrows

15

It isn't the accumulation
of all those yesterdays.

It's the sameness
of yesterday's yesterday.

It isn't the home held down
by memories and other ties.

It's the mind held back
from seeking new experiences.

It isn't the void left by the loss
of friends and lovers.

It's the turning away from the new
in favor of the comfortable.

It isn't the breakdown
of mind and body.

It's the passive acceptance
of the breakdowns

and the active pursuit of
no more tomorrows.

In The Ward

They lay like fallen leaves
Wrinkled and spotted
With colors already fading in the sun

They lay like fallen heroes
Bodies and faces
Contorted and writhing on the ground.

They lay like fallen bodies
Closer to the grave
Sweating and straining to resist that final descent.

And in their final moments
Before they turn to dust
The leaves heroic body of work
Became fuel for the next new delicate shoots.

Tremors

17

The aftershocks of death
Lay out a changed world
With hidden rifts
And continental drifts
Upthrust emotions
With perilous cliffs

The aftershocks of death
Leave me unsteady on my feet
Untrusting that the ground
Is not still moving around
And Mother Earth's skin
Won't splatter me down

The aftershocks of death
Leave me in a changed body
Fault lines pulled tight
Shifting ruins in the night
My mind in a chasm
Searching for light

The aftershocks of death
Leave me with an altered heart
Skip-stopping the beat
An irregular repeat
Trying to continue while
Missing you
Missing you
Missing you

Streaming the Styx

My dining room lit by a tablet.
A touch of a finger sends content
Streaming hundreds of miles
Only to stop short.
Pixels pulse in electronic agony;
My Father's funeral under glass.
Voices of prayers,
Voices of praise,
Voices of his past
All expressed,
Compressed,
And digitally re-addressed
Trying to pour out a poor set of speakers
Where only painful imagination
Can bring them to life.
Vaulted ceiling reduced
To a flat 6x8 screen.
Not a breath of air gets through.
No scents or sense of it all.
Surreal, unreal, and playable
Over and over and over.

Possessions

The last years of my parents' life
Had seen their possessions reduced
And scattered across several states.
From a place of multi-stories
Their home shrunk to a single story
And then just an apartment,
Mingling in multiple shared stories.
They held onto the lake place
With it's view of Mother's dreams
While furniture and memories
Were packed away and parceled out
To kids, grandkids, and Goodwill.
The last move, to assisted living,
Brought them down to the ground
Floor in a completely different state.
Mother slipped away taking only
Her funeral dress, glasses, and a rosary.
Her other belongings were gone
A heartbreaking heartbeat later.
When Father's last breath
Left his body and became simply air,
My Sister was there to receive his last
Mortal possession, his body,
Later buried with Mother and marked
On a map like a treasure.

Blizzard

The flurry of activity at your death
Turns into a blizzard of decisions
At times icing over to freeze us in our tracks.
Relentlessly the cold reality marches onward
As one by one we break a path forward
Through the trackless drifts of days ahead.
Across this new wilderness we call out to each other
Finding our own path to come together.
There is only one destination that can save us.
Only one way to make it through.
Clinging together for warmth
We slowly make our way home.

Riverchild

I am pulled forward by my parents' current,
bobbing along carefree as a child,
learning the strokes as a teen,
stretching and strengthening myself
as a young adult.
Their deaths thrust me,
floundering and kicking,
into the riptides outside
their disappearing wake.
I learn to breathe
and pace myself
as my parents slide
under the surface,
slowly sinking
into the depths
of my past.

Comet

A new gravity is pulling me
Outward and onward
Things I used to do
I let fall away
I'm drifting from
The stable orbit of my family
Like a comet
Off on a dark journey
Into uncharted territories
Casting off pieces of itself
Sending sparks shooting
Away from the home fires

I fumble my way forward
In fits and flashes.
Behind me the double star
I orbited for so long
Compresses and crumbles
Shrinking towards
An inevitable event horizon
Leaving me to find my own way.